A Year of Christian Festivals

Flora York

W

FRANKLIN WATTS
LONDON・SYDNEY

This edition 2013

First published by Franklin Watts

Franklin Watts
338 Euston Road
LONDON NW1 3BH

Franklin Watts Australia
Level 17/207 Kent Street
Sydney NSW 2000

Dewey classification: 263'.9
ISBN: 978 1 4451 1782 9

Art Direction: Jonathan Hair
Illustrations: Peter Bull
Faith Consultant: Martin Ganeri

Designer (original edition): Joelle Wheelwright
Picture Research: Diana Morris

Produced for Franklin Watts by Storeybooks. The text of this book is based on
Christian Festivals Through the Year by Anita Ganeri © Franklin Watts 2003.

Acknowledgements
The publishers would like to thank the following for permission to reproduce
photographs in this book: Anthony Blake Photo Library/ Photothèque Culinaire: 14b;
Britstock-IFA/ HAGA: 21t; Michael Dalder/ Reuters/ Popperfoto: 19b; Dick Doughty/
Britstock-IFA/ HAGA: 13t, 25t; Bernd Ducke/ Britstock-IFA: 8t, 16b; Franklin Watts
Photo Libary: 6t, 16t, 23b, 26 (Steve Shott); 6b, 7t, 9t, 18b, 20t, 27t (Chris
Fairclough); 13b, 17t, 24b; Grant V. Faint/ The Image Bank/ Getty Images: front
cover, 15; G. Graefenhain/ Britstock-IFA: 12t; Hideo Haga/ Britstock-IFA: 8b; Atsuko
Isobe/ Britstock-IFA/ HAGA: 7c; Bruco Lucas/ Britstock-IFA: 12b; Carlos Reyes-Manzo/
Andes Press Agency: 14t, 17b, 20b, 22; Akiro Nakata/ Britstock-IFA/HAGA: 23t; A.
Diaz Neira/ Britstock-IFA: 19t; © Trip/Viesti Collection: 27b; Waldenfels/ Britstock-IFA:
24t; Heidi Weidner/ Britstock-IFA: 18t; Jennifer Woodcock/ Reflections Photo Library/
Corbis: 10; Masakatsu Yamazaki/ Britstock-IFA/HAGA: 11b. Every attempt has been
made to clear copyright. Should there be any inadvertent omission please apply to
the publisher for rectification.

Printed in China

Franklin Watts is a division of Hachette Children's Books,
an Hachette UK company.
www.hachette.co.uk

Contents

Words printed in **bold** are explained in the glossary.

Christians

Christians believe that God made our world. They believe that God had a son called Jesus Christ, who was born on Earth. When Jesus grew up, he became a **preacher** and a **healer**. He lived in the Middle East 2,000 years ago.

▲ *A painting of Jesus.*

Jesus's message

God sent Jesus to Earth to teach people how to live a good life. Jesus's teachings are written in a book called the **Bible**. Today there are Christians all over the world.

◀ *Many Christian churches have beautiful stained-glass windows.*

Churches

Christians go to church to thank and praise God, and to learn how to be good Christians.

There are many different groups of Christians, such as Protestants, Anglicans, Roman Catholics and **Orthodox** Christians.

▲ *Christians at a service in a church.*

◀ *A statue of Jesus is carried in an Easter procession in Guatemala.*

Services

In a church service, people say prayers and sing **hymns**. They listen to a talk that helps them to live a Christian life. There are also special services to mark things that are important to Christians.

Christian festivals

Festivals are special times when Christians gather together. They meet to mark or **celebrate** events in Jesus's life, or important times in Christian history, and to give thanks to God. There may be church services, **ceremonies** and food. People may give gifts.

Advent

Christians celebrate the birth of Jesus on Christmas Day, 25 December. The four weeks before Christmas are called Advent. The word means 'arrival' or 'coming' and is talking about the arrival of Jesus.

An Advent market in ▶ Germany.

◀ *An Advent service.*

Advent Sunday

During Advent, Christians think about Jesus's birth. The first Sunday of Advent is called Advent Sunday. Many Christians go to a special service in church.

Advent ring

Some churches have a ring of candles to light during Advent. There are four candles around the outside, and one is lit on each Sunday of Advent. There is another candle in the centre, which is lit on Christmas Day.

The candles stand for Jesus, and the hope he brought to all people in the world.

◀ *Lighting a candle on an Advent ring.*

Advent calendar

Make an Advent calendar to mark off the days before Christmas.

1. Draw a picture of Jesus's birth (see p. 10) on a large sheet of card.

2. Draw 24 numbered windows on top (make window 24 the biggest). Score around three sides of each window so it can be opened.

3. Place the window card on top of a second piece of card (same size). Open the windows carefully and draw around them on the second piece of card.

4. On the second piece of card, put a picture in each of the boxes you have drawn. (Draw your own or cut from old Christmas cards.)

5. Spread glue along the edge of the second card and place the first card on top. (Make sure the glue doesn't go as far as the windows.)

6. Shut the windows. Starting on 1 December, open one window each day to show a picture.

Christmas

No one knows exactly when Jesus was born, but Christians celebrate his birthday on 25 December.

Orthodox Christians follow a different calendar, and have Christmas Day on 7 January.

Jesus's parents

Jesus's parents were **Jewish** people called Mary and Joseph. They lived in a country that we now call Israel.

The Bible says that an angel called Gabriel told Mary she was going to have a baby. The baby would be the son of God and he would save people and give them a new life.

Jesus is born

Mary and Joseph had to travel to **Bethlehem** to pay their taxes. They couldn't find anywhere to stay and had to spend the night in a stable. There Jesus was born. Soon afterwards, shepherds and three kings came to the stable to **worship** Jesus.

▲ *Children acting out the story of Jesus's birth. This is called a nativity play.*

Christmas in church

On Christmas Eve, many churches hold a special service called Midnight Mass. On Christmas Day, people go to church to sing **carols** and thank God for sending Jesus to them.

A Christingle

'Christingle' means 'Christ light'. Make a Christingle as a decoration.

1. Push a small candle into the top of an orange.
2. Add four cocktail sticks with nuts, raisins and sweets pushed on them.
3. Tie a red ribbon around the orange.

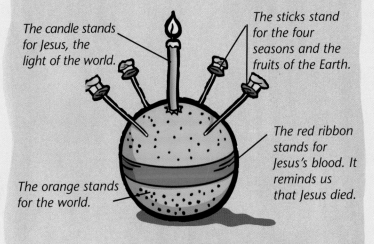

The candle stands for Jesus, the light of the world.

The sticks stand for the four seasons and the fruits of the Earth.

The red ribbon stands for Jesus's blood. It reminds us that Jesus died.

The orange stands for the world.

St Lucia's Day

In Sweden, Christmas celebrations begin on St Lucia's Day. Legend says that Lucia helped protect the early Christians. She was later made a **saint**. ('Saint' can be shortened to 'St'.) On this day, girls dress as Lucia. They wear a white dress and a crown of leaves and candles.

◀ *Girls on St Lucia's Day, 13 December.*

Christmas customs

Christians have special **customs** at Christmas. In some countries, they may put up Christmas trees and decorations, send cards and presents, and enjoy Christmas food. People who are not Christians also like to do these things.

▲ *Christmas on the beach!*

Christmas presents

The three kings who visited baby Jesus took him presents of gold, frankincense and myrrh. Christians give gifts to remember this, and also that Jesus was God's gift to the world.

In the Netherlands, children receive their presents on 6 December, St Nicholas's Day. A legend says that Saint Nicholas, or Sinterklaas (Santa Claus), was a **bishop** who lived in Myra, Turkey.

St Stephen's Day

Saint Stephen was killed for teaching people about Jesus. St Stephen's Day is the day after Christmas Day. In Britain, it is also called Boxing Day. In the past, boxes of money, clothes and food were shared among the poor.

Christmas dinner

Christmas pudding is made from dried fruit.

On Christmas Day in Britain and many other places, lots of people eat roast turkey followed by Christmas pudding. In some countries, the special Christmas meal is on Christmas Eve. In Italy, fish with lentils is a favourite. In Poland, poppy seed cake and beetroot soup are popular.

Epiphany

Twelve days after Christmas, it is Epiphany. This is on 6 January and celebrates the three kings' visit to baby Jesus in the stable in Bethlehem. It also celebrates Jesus's **baptism**.

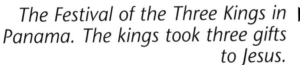

The Festival of the Three Kings in Panama. The kings took three gifts to Jesus. ▶

Three Kings' Day

In Spain, Epiphany is called Three Kings' Day. Children receive their Christmas presents on this day. The night before, they leave out their shoes for the kings to fill with gifts.

◀ *In many countries, people bake a Twelfth Night cake. It may have gifts or money inside.*

Candlemas

The festival of Candlemas celebrates an important event in baby Jesus's life (see below). It takes place 40 days after Christmas, on 2 February. Some churches hold a special service.

Candles

The word 'Candlemas' comes from the Roman Catholic Church. It was traditional for a priest to **bless** candles on 2 February for use during the year. Some Roman Catholic churches still have candlelit processions.

▲ Candles remind us that Jesus is a guiding light.

The Temple in Jerusalem

The Temple was a very special building where the Jewish people went to worship God.

When a baby boy was 40 days old, his parents took him to the Temple and gave thanks to God.

Mary and Joseph took Jesus to the Temple when he was this age. The festival of Candlemas remembers this time.

The festival is also known as The Presentation of the Lord.

Lent

When Jesus grew up, he began to teach people about God. But Jesus had lots of enemies who wanted to get rid of him. Eventually, they killed him. But two days later, Jesus came back to life!

Jesus was killed by being nailed to a ▶ wooden cross. Many churches have models or statues of this.

▼ *A carnival in Brazil.*

The start of Lent

The 40 days before Easter are called Lent. During this time, Christians think about Jesus's death.

The day before Lent is called Shrove Tuesday or Mardi Gras. Many countries have a carnival. There are processions through the streets with singers and dancers.

Fasting

Jesus was baptised when he was about 30. Then he spent 40 days in the desert without food. The Devil tried to get Jesus to worship him, but Jesus refused.

In Lent, people used to fast, or go without food, like Jesus did. Many people still give up treats such as sweets.

Pancake Day

In Lent, Christians traditionally ate plain, simple food. So on Shrove Tuesday, they had to use up rich foods such as fat, eggs and milk. In Britain, these ingredients were made into pancakes.

That is why Shrove Tuesday is often called Pancake Day.

Ash Wednesday

The first day of Lent is called Ash Wednesday. In Roman Catholic churches, the priest makes a cross with ash on each person's forehead. The ash is a sign that people are sorry for the wrong things that they have done.

Mothering Sunday

This is on the fourth Sunday of Lent. In church, there are prayers to thank mothers for all their hard work. People give flowers and a card to their mother.

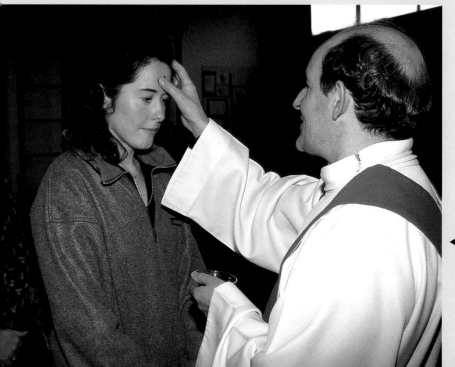

◄ *A priest makes an ash cross on the forehead.*

Holy Week

The last week of Lent is Holy Week. It starts with Palm Sunday and ends with Easter Sunday. At this time, Christians think about the last week of Jesus's life.

Palm Sunday

On Palm Sunday, Jesus rode into **Jerusalem** on a donkey. Crowds of people waved palm branches to welcome him. Today, people are given small palm-leaf crosses in church to remind them of that day.

▲ *On Palm Sunday in Germany, people are given catkin twigs.*

The Last Supper

Jesus ate a last meal with his **disciples** because he knew he was going to die. Jesus gave them bread and wine, which he said were his body and his blood. Today, there are services called Mass, Holy Communion, or the **Eucharist**. These happen throughout the year. In this service, people have bread and wine to remember Jesus.

◄ *The minister, vicar or priest blesses the bread and wine for Communion.*

Maundy Thursday

'Maundy' means 'a command'. On this day, at the Last Supper, Jesus told his disciples to keep meeting to share bread and wine after his death, and to love one another. He showed his love for them by washing their feet.

A Holy Week procession in Spain. The clothes are a sign of sadness. ▶

Good Friday

On Friday of Holy Week, Jesus died on the cross. This sad day is called Good Friday because Christians believe that Jesus died for the good of all the people on Earth.

On Good Friday, Christians may eat hot cross buns. The cross on the top is a reminder of the way that Jesus died.

◀ *Actors telling the story of Holy Week. Jesus had to carry the cross that he was to die on.*

Easter Sunday

On Easter Sunday, Jesus came back to life. It is a very important day for Christians, and a happy time. Churches have a special Easter service to thank God for Jesus's life. They are often decorated with flowers.

Jesus lives

When Jesus died, he was put in a tomb with a huge stone across the entrance. Later, his friends found the tomb was empty. Jesus had come back to life and gone.

Easter vigil

Roman Catholics have a special service called the Easter vigil, which starts outside the church. A big Easter candle called the Paschal is lit, then everyone lights a small candle from this and walks into the church singing a hymn.

Lighting the Paschal ▶ at an Easter vigil in South Africa.

Easter eggs

Giving eggs at Easter celebrates new life. Christians remember how Jesus came back to life. But eggs also **symbolise** springtime.

▲ At Easter, there are sometimes competitions where eggs are used, like this one in America.

Decorated eggs

Try decorating some eggs to use as an Easter decoration.

1. Ask an adult to cook some hard-boiled eggs. Leave them to cool.

2. Draw a pattern on the shell with a wax crayon. Dip the egg in a bowl of food colouring. It will stain the shell, except where the pattern appears.

3. Or just use paints to paint a design. You could even make the eggs look like people.

Easter meaning

Christians believe that Jesus came back to life to show that when we die, it is not the end of everything. Instead it is the start of a new life with God.

Summer festivals

Ascension Day

When Jesus came back to life, he stayed on Earth for 40 days. Then he went to **heaven** to be with God for ever. This day is called Ascension Day.

▲ *People are often baptised at Pentecost. This is a baptism in Africa.*

Pentecost

At Pentecost, a strong wind blew through the house in Jerusalem where Jesus's disciples were praying, and they were filled with the spirit of God (see below). They went out and started teaching people about Jesus. Today, Christians see Pentecost as the start of the Christian Church. The festival is 50 days after Easter.

Trinity Sunday

The Sunday after Pentecost is called Trinity Sunday. 'Trinity' means 'three'. Christians believe that God is one god, who is:
• God the Father who made and cares for the world;
• God the Son, who came to Earth as Jesus;
• God the Holy Spirit, the power of God (God at work in the world).

Corpus Christi

This Roman Catholic festival celebrates the Last Supper. Catholics believe that the bread people eat during Mass is the body of Jesus Christ. At Corpus Christi, the bread is carried through the streets in a procession. Some people kneel as the bread goes past, to show their respect.

▲ *A Corpus Christi procession in Italy. The ground is scattered with flowers.*

The Assumption

On 15 August, Roman Catholics remember Mary, Jesus's mother. At the end of her life, she was taken up into heaven. The word 'Assumption' here means 'being taken up'. In the Orthodox Church, this festival is called the Dormition. It means 'the falling asleep'.

◀ *A painting of Mary and Jesus.*

Harvest festivals

Harvest time is when farmers bring in the crops that are ready to eat.

Many churches hold a harvest festival to thank God for all the plants that give us food. Churches are decorated with flowers, fruit and vegetables.

▲ *The fruit and vegetable decorations in church are later given to charities.*

Harvest meal

In Britain, harvest festival is in autumn, but in other countries it may be at a different time. Some churches hold a harvest lunch or supper. People gather together to enjoy a delicious meal and thank God for all the food that we eat.

◄ *A harvest loaf in the shape of a sheaf of wheat.*

Thanksgiving

The first settlers arrived in the USA almost 400 years ago. When they harvested their first crops, the settlers gratefully thanked God. This is how Thanksgiving day got its name.

In November, Americans celebrate Thanksgiving with a meal of turkey.

▲ *An American family enjoying a Thanksgiving dinner.*

A harvest banner

In many churches there are special fabric pictures called banners. These are hung up at different times of year.

1. Try making a harvest banner. Cut a rectangle of plain, fairly stiff cloth. Turn over the edges, and sew or stick them down.

2. Cut different scraps of cloth into shapes to do with the harvest, such as fruit, vegetables and corn. Sew or stick them on to the banner.

A harvest hymn

We plough the fields,
and scatter
The good seed on the land,
But it is fed and watered
By God's almighty hand.
He sends the snow in winter,
The warmth to swell the grain,
The breezes and the sunshine,
And soft, refreshing rain.
All good gifts around us
Are sent from heaven above.
Then thank the Lord,
O thank the Lord,
For all his love.

Saints and souls

The **Church** can decide to make an especially good or **holy** person into a saint. Each saint has a special day in the year on which he or she is remembered, as well as on All Saints' Day.

Patron saints are linked with particular things. For example, Saint Christopher is the patron saint of travellers.

All Saints' Day

Christians celebrate All Saints' Day to give thanks for all the saints and the good things that they did.

Some Christians celebrate on 1 November. Orthodox Christians celebrate in June.

▼ *Pictures of saints in an Orthodox Christian church.*

The soul

Christians believe that a soul is the invisible part of a person that remains after he or she has died. The soul goes to heaven to live with God.

All Souls' Day is the day after All Saints' Day.

▲ *In many countries, people place flowers on the graves of their loved ones.*

All Souls' Day

On All Souls' Day, Christians remember people in their family who have died, and pray for them.

In Mexico, this day is called the Day of the Dead. People visit cemeteries with food and model skulls.

◀ *These sugar skulls have been made for Day of the Dead celebrations in Mexico.*

Festival calendar

Date	Month	Event
	November/December	Advent Sunday
6	December	St Nicholas's Day
13	December	St Lucia's Day
25	December	Christmas Day
26	December	St Stephen's Day/Boxing Day
6	January	Epiphany
7	January	Christmas Day (Orthodox)
2	February	Candlemas
	February/March	Shrove Tuesday
	February/March	Lent
	March/April	Mothering Sunday
	March/April	Holy Week: Palm Sunday, Maundy Thursday, Good Friday, Holy Saturday, Easter Sunday
	April/May	Ascension Day
	May/June	Pentecost/Whitsun
	May/June	Trinity Sunday
	May/June	Corpus Christi
15	August	Feast of the Assumption Dormition (Orthodox)
	September/October	Harvest festival
1	November	All Saints' Day
2	November	All Souls' Day
	November	Thanksgiving Day (USA)

Glossary

Baptism A ceremony at which a person becomes a full member of the Christian Church. The person is sprinkled with water (or bathed in water) to wash away the wrong things he or she has done.

Bethlehem A town in Israel where Jesus was born.

Bible The Christians' holy book. It is made up of the Old Testament and the New Testament. The Old Testament dates back to before Jesus was born. The New Testament contains the life and words of Jesus.

Bishop A church minister in charge of the churches in one area.

Bless To say special words to thank or worship God, or make something holy. The words can also ask God to protect someone or something.

Carol A hymn or song that people sing at Christmas.

Celebrate To be pleased and happy about something, and to have special festivities to mark the occasion.

Ceremonies Occasions when you do special things to mark an event.

Church A church is a place where people go to worship God. 'The Church' means the Christian religion. It can also mean a group of Christians, such as the Roman Catholic Church, or the Orthodox Church.

Customs Habits or traditions.

Disciples The twelve men chosen by Jesus to be his close friends and followers.

Eucharist The service at which people have bread and wine to remember Jesus. It is also called Mass or Holy Communion.

Healer Someone who cures people of illness.

Heaven Where God lives. Christians believe we go to heaven when we die.

Holy Something to do with God. A person who is holy is extremely good and dedicated to God.

Hymns Songs that praise God.

Jerusalem A city in Israel where Jesus died.

Jewish A Jew is a person whose religion is Judaism. Jesus's family were Jewish and he was born and raised as a Jew.

Orthodox A type of faith or Christian group that follows religious laws and practices that were set out by the early Christian Church.

Preacher A person who talks to others about God, the Christian religion and the way God wants people to live their life.

Saint A person who the Church decides is especially good or holy.

Symbolise To stand for something else. An Easter egg is a symbol of new life.

Worship To show love and respect for Jesus or God.

Further resources

Websites

www.jesusandkidz.com
American site with illustrated Bible stories.

http://atschool.eduweb.co.uk/ carolrb/christianity/index.html
Christianity and Christian festivals.

www.stmarkorthodox.org/ kids.html
American site with information about the Orthodox Church.

http://methodist.org.uk/static/ children/children/home.htm
Bible stories, jokes, things to do.

www.christian-kids.net
Prayers, games and bible extracts.

Note to parents and teachers: Every effort has been made by the Publishers to ensure that these websites are suitable for children, that they are of the highest educational value, and that they contain no inappropriate or offensive material. However, because of the nature of the Internet, it is impossible to guarantee that the contents of these sites will not be altered. We strongly advise that Internet access is supervised by a responsible adult.

Index